THERE WILL BE DANCING

ALSO BY KEMAL HOUGHTON

Lizard (1983)

Pastizzi (Cestria, 2011)

There Will Be Dancing

Kemal Houghton

Poems

To Amy

May you always find room to dance

[illegible]

14/6/23

RED SQUIRREL PRESS

First published in 2020 by Red Squirrel Press
36 Elphinstone Crescent
Biggar
South Lanarkshire
ML12 6GU
www.redsquirrelpress.com

Edited by David J Costello

Typesetting and design by Gerry Cambridge
e:gerrycambridge@btinternet.com

Cover artwork: LaInspiratriz/shutterstock.com

ISBN: 978 1 913632 0 14

A CIP catalogue record is available from the British Library.

Red Squirrel Press is committed to a sustainable future. This pamphlet is printed in Scotland by Love & Humphries using Forest Stewardship Council certified paper.
www.loveandprint.co.uk

Contents

For Caroline, more than a partner

A Sense of Purpose

The purpose of this morning
is to slide the hours
into the afternoon
with the constant swish
of performance indicators
falling
without
reason
past the third-floor window.

The day is brisk
with autumn air
on distant hills.

The purpose of this morning
is to let the sun
rise high
above this building
and drag its shadow
from one side
to the other.

The gulls fly
westward,
making for the sea.

The purpose of this morning
is to make the space
wide enough for all
this drudgery to slip
into place and settle
in the dusty vaults
of the brain.

A dead man scrapes
at the windowpane—
not yet allocated
to his place
in heaven
or hell.

Advice to Lot's Wife

Once you've decided what to do,
get on with it! Do not spend too
long on desert corners thinking
about ethics, reasons and things;
there are none to be found there. When
under such scrutiny, even
the best ideas will turn to stone.
Just pack your tent and go (alone
if necessary) and don't ask
questions that you don't need to ask.
If you should hear the roar of fire
close behind, ignore it. Don't tire
of running 'til the race is through,
there will be time enough for you
to ask those questions and maybe
think up some answers then. Don't be
tempted by paths that lead away
from Zoar if that is where you say
you're going. Don't be petrified
in the hot vastness when the wide
plain surrounds you, nor be conformed
by cities where your brain is pawned
to pay the rent. Now, if you're set
on going, hurry and don't let
doubts stand in your way. Keep wisdom
at your side. Then, when the sounds from
the cities stop you in your tracks,
above all else, please don't look back.

The Time Fairy

The Time Fairy
removes the hours
from busy days
and dumps them
in places
you least want to be.

She steals whole weeks
in the run-up to Christmas
then spreads them,
a dark slush
in the lassitude
of the winter's night.

She snatches time
from the lips
of parting lovers
on railway platforms
everywhere. Then
you may see her
skipping round bus queues,
especially in the rain,
sprinkling them
with minutes,
hours
and lengthening grim faces
on autumn homeward journeys.

Gardeners know her
best as they await
their most prized blooms,
for all about
the weeds grow double-quick

in lengthened mornings
sparkled with dew.

Her meanest trick
is to the old
whose years flash
as a day,
but to the very young
she gives an age
between each high
or holiday.

The Time Fairy:
she wrings the moments
from all life's pleasures
and drips them into
the waiting hours
when we are most desolate
and wanting.

Every Drop

I am the drip that wears the stone,
darkly I fill the upland wastes,
then trickle the hillside where I
crash and fall. I am the roar
at the valley's heart where I sing
my song as I dash to be free.

I am the green upon the lawn,
the juice that feeds the forest pine,
each little sip the sparrow takes,
each cup of tea, each cask of wine.

Trapped underground, I have distilled
the years where I've been the maker
of caverns and spires. Caught out by
the cold at the roof of the world
or at the Earth's poles where I turn
so solid I can crush the rocks.

Your great ships may cruise me, careless
you've abused me as you clutter
the oceans with pain. But I am
the one drop inside your collar
who'll shudder a chill down your spine.

Tougher than Belfast steel, I am
heavier than the air you breathe;
I am the force that can sweep you
away. I will rise and fill up
these fields, drown your crops and livestock;
this planet has always been mine.

From the stiffness in the plant's stem,
the liquid in the blood, I float
all the things you do and I am
always
          the better part of you.

Music

He once played the clarinet
like generations before
but, by the time I knew him,
he didn't have the teeth for it
and that finely tuned ear
that had led the Sunday School Choir
had become numbed by almost
forty years of clanging
in the shipyard din.
But rhythm—
he could listen to an engine
and tell you to a stroke
if the mixture was too rich,
the piston rings too worn,
the big-ends about to go.
That was his music.
He couldn't make out
the muffled slur
of the gramophone,
"Drunken men singing
through keyholes" his father-in-law
had called it, and he'd agreed.
Where other sounds
lost their sense to him,
the engine's steady pulse
still remained. Whether it was
a ship or some old Ford,
a locomotive or static in a mill,
he'd worked them all
and knew their scales.
He was small enough
to climb into spaces
that other men could never reach

and so he became intimate
with the metal and the thrust
of it all. And nothing
could beat the fine tuning
with feelers and the subtle flinch
of tiny screws coaxing
some sullen block
into a crescendo of life.
Then he'd stand there, listening,
humming to its song.

Electric Minstrel

Plugged-in and tunes selected,
the electric minstrel fills the air
with a beat they will know
and a voice that must coax.
Some may glance her way
in the lull of conversations,
but she is the salt of the diners;
the liquid of the glass.
Her mother was a jukebox,
her father played the fiddle.
Long ago there was someone
playing a lute while people, as always,
shouted over the racket.

Her job is to entertain,
distract and take away the silence.
She is in every town, every encampment,
wherever people have knotted together.
She drives through the rain, as she always has,
down mud-spattered lanes
with carts or whatever could be carried
on groaning backs. And this road is no place
for the squeamish. Many have fallen; Buddy Holly,
Johnny Kidd, Eddie Cochran are just a few.

Yet she will battle above the rows,
the women who teeter towards a fight
and the drunken laughter. She
will get their attention.
Now someone is singing in the corner,
bodies unwittingly move to the beat.
They have learned to accept her voice
and there will be dancing.

Sister

My sister is a red dust road;
the back-to-backs of Birkenhead,
a puzzle that remains untold

hid in the lining we have sewed
about our core with unseen threads.
My sister is a red dust road

stretched from a distant land of old
to reach this place we cannot shed;
a puzzle that remains untold

which binds us and does not corrode
despite the tangled paths we tread.
My sister is a red dust road

that sways and sings an unknown ode
from Africa to Birkenhead;
a puzzle that remains untold.

We grew together, though not bred
by parents who might well have said
my sister is a red dust road;
a puzzle that remains untold.

Red Dust Road (Pan Macmillan UK, 2010) is the title of Jackie Kay's autobiography which tells of her search for her birth parents in Scotland and Nigeria.

Translation

In the Citroen listening
to Piaf, the snow thickening
as we drive towards
the hills. And you humming along,
with the winter sun bright
on the fields; sky enigmatic blue.
We cross the border,
mark how the river
has been displaced.
Traffic is sparse
but slow. The moorland
whited out. At the top
of the pass we stop, leave the car
and follow a fox's footprints
up the hill. The world
below pure as
a wedding gown;
your blushed cheek.
Later we explore
charity shops,
try our hand at translating
from the Welsh the sign
above the card shop by the bridge
and realise
we already know
what it means;
there is no need to explain.

Babel: Hotel and Flights

After that first package holiday
he talked about the poverty,
people who still farmed by hand,
whose greatest possession
was a donkey, and that
half broken.

He told them all about the flight,
how the plane went above the clouds
so high that they looked like
stuffing ripped from a mattress
far below.

"And did you see the angels?"
his mother asked. "No, no
I didn't see them." He went on
with his story, fallen—almost sorry.

His father was already lost,
struggling with the metaphysics
of it all, but his mother
never had the language.
His little brother soon got bored
and went off to play.
His sister confirmed that
going up in aeroplanes
was silly.

X-Ray Specs

At first he used them
to see through
girls' clothes,
but only saw
their lungs,
the odd broken bone,
their hearts pumping.

He wanted to use them
to fix things:
to see the workings
of his dad's car—
make it go faster;
he wanted to see
where the bodies fell
behind the TV screen—
make it clearer.
But all he saw
was the tarmac beneath
or the wallpaper behind.

He focused and re-focused.
Tried to see
more and more
in every space.
He looked into the volcano
to seek out its molten source,
but he saw right through the earth
to the clear blue skies beyond.

Then he turned his gaze
towards heaven
for the smiling face
of god.

Finally, when he could
see through everything
and could stare deep
into the void beyond
the universe,
all he could find
was blackness.
He closed his eyes
and the blackness remained.

Nosferatu

There was no going back.
He had been too many people;
all flotsam in his wake.
Some had sunk into oblivion,
while others crashed
                                        with the voiceless slam
of a door;
                  a wave sprawled distant on the sand.

He knew no birth without the salt of tears
and each new life brought fear and its own ruin.
The dead could never return
          and he had given up all hope
for the lost.

                        He continued
seeking the sting of daylight,
enjoying each new version of himself,
wringing life to the full.

Now he was far away,
his former selves fading as he moved
          on and on and on.

Yet, each night he slept in a box
of his own native earth
with visions of childhood
          teasing his head,
waking each day, wasted
                      and dispossessed.

Monster

From its inception we knew
that anything without the power
of decay would one day haunt us
and our children's children
throughout the treads of time.

We saw its strength,
admired its flexibility
and moulded it to suit our own image.
Strange how we let it take over,
how it became essential
to everything we touched.

Even as it carried our shopping
we knew we could never rid ourselves
of him. If we buried him in the ground
he would always be there
                                        at the turning of a spade.

Now he hangs ghoulish from trees,
clutters the streets, spreads into
the world's farthest corners.

In the sea he floats like some overblown
oligarch, swirling with the current,
becoming his own island.

He spews on every beach,
strangles wildlife
and now becomes small enough
to drip into the food chain—
slowly poisoning his creators.

The Darkenings

They walk unseen amongst us, but
will make their presence felt as they
syphon the breath from your lungs; these
dark matter forms who occupy
the shadows. At first you will not
notice them standing next to you
at the station or by the bar.

They skulk in staffrooms, sabotage
your meetings with plausible tongues
that spew a loathsome bile on all
virile thought.

They haunt the office,
lurk in hospital corridors,
linger in church when the people
have all but gone; this way they creep
onto committees, worm their way
into friendships and become close,
so close your dreams will slowly fade.

You start to snarl at small children
crying in the street. You become
rude to waitresses who only
do their best to please. Now you must
know their stealth will surely turn you
as they drain away life's juices
from your veins.

Your world will become
one of endless gloom in a cold
and fathomless vacuity
with just the shades of former friends;
a masquerade of company.

Offa's Dyke Path: Horizons

At clear times we can see for miles,
trace the days of walking along
an arc of peaks
to a vanishing point far,
far away.

We try to name the towns snuggled
in the folds of the landscape
or strewn across the plains,
but cannot be sure.

We ask no questions of the path;
this much we have learned.
What goes down will surely come up,
and what goes up will, one day,
reach the sea.

But always I must push ahead,
climb each hill to see
where the path will lead.

We chase these horizons which,
though close,
are never close enough
and, like shadows
can never be caught.

Offa's Dyke Path: In Mist

The pace of life slows to a step
along each rugged or muddied
path. We slide in the wetness, feel
the fall of the earth beneath us.

All sense of place is muddled here
in the fog of the hills. Valleys
are lost, even the route ahead
is consumed by the fallen cloud.

Company is sparse. Huddled shapes
mist past: walkers, wild ponies, but
mostly sheep. Few words are spoken,
just the duplicitous skylark
singing us away from her nest.

Through faith we follow the way down,
markers mostly point the right way,
though some need interpretation.
Guidebooks and GPS all help.

We enter each new town the way
people have done throughout the years;
strange pilgrims in search of shelter.

To Autumn

So here you are again;
I loved you in my youth,
you had me melt into those deep brown eyes,
snuggle into your soft woollen jumpers—
your russet coat fallen on the threshing-floor.
I would taste wild berries
crushed against your lips
and, when your chill winds raged,
I could rejoin with hail and rain.

But now that I am old enough
to appreciate the softer scents of spring
and the promise of warmth she brings;
I see the swipe of your harvester
and view with suspicion
the furrows of your plough.

Doing the Cards

I am become my mother
surrounded by heaps of cards
and lists of names; a personal
Who's Who and who is not.

The faces time remembered;
time forgot. People
not spoken to in decades,
a litany of broken promises
to call.

Accusingly, the lists
begin to pall, as now
the pages fill with scratching out
loved ones whose time will not return again.

Next year I'll flick a switch,
print the addresses out, then stamp
each Christmas card with both our names.

Of Shakespeare

Here is all life played out for us to see,
From noble kings to beggars, rogues and fools,
All spun from tricks of light to fantasy
With stirrings conjured up by folly's tools.

Thus draws the wonder from the mind's cold eye
To leap at things that dreams would not believe,
Our lives suspend where fairies oft may fly
With such enchantments that we scarce perceive.

And by this guise we learn of tales that teach
How constant human nature has remained.
We know too well these characters, for each
We analyse holds true to some less famed.

Now, as the lights dim from our little show
We leave engraced by all we've come to know.

Acknowledgements

The following poems first appeared in other publications:
'A Sense of Purpose' was published in *Poetry Scotland 60* and *Habitats of the Mind* (Cestrian Press 2010);
'Advice to Lot's Wife' was published in Chester Poets 8 (Cestrian Press 1981);
'The Time Fairy' was published online by *Three Drops of the Cauldron* and in *Spaces* (Cestrian Press 2012);
'Music' was published in *Life Begins* (Cestrian Press 2014);
'Translation' was published in *Poetry Scotland 92*;
'X-Ray Specs' was published in *Habitats of the Mind* (Cestrian Press 2010);
'To Autumn' was published in *Spaces* (Cestrian Press 2012);
'Of Shakespeare' was published in *Unheard* (Cestrian Press 2016).

Thanks are due to the Chester Poets, the Pop-up Poets, First Thursday and Poetry Scotland for all their encouragement over the years, to David J. Costello for his attention to detail and thoughtful editorship, friends and family and especially my wife, Caroline, who continually spurs me on.

A NOTE ON THE TYPE

This pamphlet is set in Goudy Modern Pro, a contemporary updating of the American type designer Frederick W. Goudy's highly distinctive serif of 1915.